To My ...

May this Book empower

you & yours

Morality

The Quantum Consciousness Of Being

by
Dwayne Gavin

Powerful lessons filled with personal insights and skills to develop the awareness of your inner self. It is a wellspring of unlimited intelligence, the place where morality is born.

© Copyright, 2012
By
Dwayne Gavin

ISBN: 978-1-935802-07-5

All rights reserved. No part of this publication may be reproduced, stored in a retrieval system, or transmitted in any form or by any means, electronic, mechanical, photocopying, recording, or otherwise, without the prior written permission of the publisher.

Cover design by Dominion Multi-Media, Tallahassee, Florida

Photography by Phillip Williams

Editors:
Jacqueline Harper
Natalie Perfetti
Dr. Brenda Lane-Smith

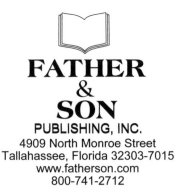

**FATHER
&
SON**
PUBLISHING, INC.
4909 North Monroe Street
Tallahassee, Florida 32303-7015
www.fatherson.com
800-741-2712

Preface

With certainty, we must remove all the opinion from around the pure soul. The soul contains all the answers to the destiny of our lives. The moment after we have gotten in touch with the precious soul, we can have the experience of finding what God has placed within us. All I have ever known is that the component to wholesomeness is the cement within our souls holding lives together.

The outlines you will gather in my book may aid you to open yourself up to many of the biblical texts, quote from contributors of the Bible and dynamic inspiration from the Spirit of the Almighty. In studying the truths gathered in this book, you will likely, expand your imagination and realize that reality depends on your identification of the things that you have been taught to accept.

I teach that reality comes to a full circle by escalated perception. It can always move to a greater state of awareness. I do not advocate a futuristic peace; instead, an immediate peace that comes from a perception within you of the world that you can prepare. By changing your perception, you also change the results of your emotions, your feelings, and well being;

therefore, peace within becomes a matter of how you are perceiving the world that you have prepared in your mind and heart.

Sections of this book will disseminate a summation for which you can overcome many handed-down versions of traditional norms, customs, and beliefs. Also, you may find these strategies preparations for talking points and initiation for higher dialogue.

Acknowledgments

For all the love and support that all of you have given me, I am appreciative. Thank you for exhibited love and support over the years.

To every one of the persons who ever offered me instructions, support, and love during any time that I have needed you, truly I thank you so much for being in my life. This book would not have the wisdom that it contains without so many good people standing alongside me and sharing with me.

Introduction

Morality: The Quantum Consciousness of Being is written especially for you, the reader. It is designed to awaken your knowing about enhancing your life. Writing this book with the flavor of understanding what all of us must find out about ourselves was my appetite for it. Within it, there are several aspects of wisdom that offers all of us a more abundant life.

What an awesome awareness and wisdom about getting to know yourself in ways that you may or may not have been taught growing up! Certainly, growing up is a lifelong project. There has always existed a journey that provides you all the explanations for your choices in life. The contents of the journey on which this book takes you are categorized as self analyses.

All human beings are unique and individually driven by the passion of life. Some basic strategies that can provide you favorable outcomes are outlined in this book. These self analyses make you aware of your heightened potential. As you delve into the wisdom about yourself in this book, my hope is that you become a more accomplished person.

You may find this book to be your very own reservoir of insights that will help you as you begin to understand who you are and what possession of power you have. It is then that your life will begin to unfold many extraordinary yet successful outcomes.

As I have longed to contribute insight to people as uninformed about themselves as I once was, I perceived with a quiet hope that merely a divine speck of self-awareness would increase their knowing. Hopefully, this increase knowing will help you position yourself in life with a clear direction, and to some degree, attain balance, power, and control. Furthermore, I aspire to bring to the surface the secret, subterranean energies that lie within all of us.

There exists at our core being such an energy that, if used, can bring about quantum leaps of consciousness that offer many heightened discoveries. At this level of consciousness, there lies *miraculous ability*. All the ability of God resides within our accepting an awareness of it. I have long believed self esteem, self empowerment, self actualization, and oneness of the self and God would put us on the path of success. Above all, there are specks of awareness in this book that will equip you with the knowing about yourself which will advance your life. So now, take this journey by reading the book. Enjoy!

Contents

1	Morality and Idiosyncrasy	1
2	Morality and Transition	5
3	Morality and Spirituality	11
4	Morality and Prayer	17
5	Morality and the Inner Self	21
6	Morality and Reconciliation	27
7	Morality and Clarity	33
8	Morality and Perspective	39
9	Morality and Happiness	43
10	Morality and Death	49
11	Summary	53
12	Epilogue	57
13	Insights of Dr. Dwayne Gavin	59
14	Bibliography	65

1
Morality and Idiosyncrasy

To the degree of perfection, there is a quality of being in accord with a system of ideas that improve morals.

It is essential that some emphasis be placed on the intelligence from which we as human beings derive our morals. It is equally important to understand how morals are born if we are to get a grip on any corrective measure to ensure reform and progression to the height of human nature at its best quality.

Moralistically speaking, I have been concerned with how human beings can extend their reach into a grander perspective for much needed reform should we someday display our best virtuous conduct. I am the first to admit that standards of morality today have to improve for there to be transcendence according to the way we view right and wrong.

To a great measurement, demoralization lurks around the lack of understanding how to correct oneself in terms of the inability of other attempts to reverse ignorance about the quality of being. As you know, many have attached morality to the soul's struggle to achieve salvation. A return visit to the soul for a correct view of right and wrong will transcend today's standard of morality. Upon this premise, the enlightened being is awakened.

There was a Master Teacher by the name of Jesus Christ who is believed to be the Redeemer, Savior, and Messiah of the world. Mostly, His ministry was characterized by issues including human and divine morals, human and divine ethics, human and spiritual character. Largely, Jesus Christ pointed His followers to a deeper morality, transition, inner self, spirituality, reconciliation, clarity, and perspective.

If you have ever looked closely at the teachings of Jesus, His sayings are simple and for many, paradoxical. For example, He was noted for teaching in parables. Within the parables of Jesus Christ, the message urged His followers to take a deeper look at the concept of morality. The divine message in the parables was intended to open the imagination of their inner selves and to provide them a revelation of clarity. With this clarity, they could reconsider their understanding about handed-down outlooks from past generations while seeing an individual need to realign their inner selves with purer reality of truth and accordingly make adjustments to their perspective. Jesus' most frequently used saying, which can help me provide you with some insight on the intention to create inner self awareness, is *"The kingdom of Heaven is like unto..."*

There are considerable aims that Jesus Christ conveyed for equipping His followers as He prepared their hearts to receive the highest human perspective on the ideology of morality. Often, His message pointed to kingdom morality. Interestingly, to have an understanding of Jesus' teachings about kingdom morality, we must understand that He pointed not to a future time line; rather, He pointed His followers to look closer at how to correct the times by saying unto them, *"The kingdom of Heaven is within you!"* This radical saying suggests, within human beings, heart and mind bring about transition according to awareness. Perfection is the action of awareness if our actions advance according to heightened awareness.

Waiting for the world to change is another way of saying that the world changes when human beings change their perspective of the world being imagined. In a very real way, the materiality of the world is as it is perceived. I will talk more about the world as something material rather than its being total essence, which can be interpreted as its source.

In terms of raising one's awareness about *heightened morality* being a divine type of morality, I have Jesus to thank. There are other spiritual paradigms for which I have a love as well. There are other truths and perspectives that I acknowledge as authentic in all ideologies and philosophies. I, however, focus on the teachings and sayings of Jesus Christ being *"The kingdom of Heaven is...."* as they internalize inner preparation and conditioning instead of waiting for an automatic transition in a dispensation of another life. Moving toward a moral perfection is a present option instead of an eschatological event pointing to another time period.

I have discovered that time, which is an item that human beings engage to construct their identification of things coming and going from their lives, often regulates their perception. This time is a matter of perception. The prerequisite to attaining heightened morality is a matter of achieving limitless awareness instead of waiting for an automatic shifting of time.

Reestablishing His Kingdom, Jesus contended with rebellion and unwillingness of His followers as He attempted to open their minds to a new way of perceiving.

As we are put here to live on earth, dominion being assigned to us by God, sovereignty, therefore, lies within us, and the way thereof is the manner in which we perceive.

2
Morality and Transition

Life takes on meaning after you have conviction about what you hold to be true and evident.

Heightened morality can be seen in a deeper way as we interact with belief. For there to be transition from one reality to a purer one, we have to see reality as steps that are ever being climbed. Human beings must engage in a lifetime of moving up the degree of awareness to discover new beliefs. Through believing, transition happens, I would like to coin the sayings, *"Individual truth is individual belief. Belief can do two things: it regulates reality and it takes on new discoveries of evidence. They are both one and the same because belief heals depending on what you believe and/or need to believe. We are constantly making significant improvement in reality when dealing with the subject of transition."*

The more you go up the latter of awareness, the more you discover new understanding with the things in life. Doing so increases new clarity with which to believe; thus, a transition takes place with your perspective of the world including yourself and others.

It is important to believe. Only what one believes comes alive within oneself. To put it simply, whether you believe the positive or the negative components of wholesomeness, it becomes alive. If you believe walking across the street, the dog is going to bite you, you will identify with having been bitten psychologically and emotionally, or if you believe that if he is not going to bite you, you cannot identify with having been bitten psychologically and emotionally.

Jesus Christ, when demonstrating the act of healing, started with the saying, "Believe." Maybe these phrases can help you see my point clearly. "Do you believe that I am able?" (typically characteristic of Jesus when staging the premise for one to obtain new evidence dealing with healing or change). His reply, therefore, would be, "Corresponding to your assurance beyond anything else, I will grant you according to your belief."

For instance, when dealing with healing the broken nature of morality, it being the lack of inner wholesomeness, Jesus used the element of belief to develop the salvation of human beings. It is noted on the subject of salvation that should one believe in his heart and confess with his mouth, it shall be his to attain. Look closely at how attainment is acquired from these very simple paradoxical verses of scripture in Romans 10: 9-11. Above all, the result of believing when dealing with salvation occurs when the assurance is anchored with the elements of belief.

Passage from one form or state of mind is the type of transition I am addressing. Heightened morality is for the purpose of reaching our human height and accelerating our being to the fullest potential. Awareness transfers morality; thus, the lifelong commitment to openness to purer reality is the height of human be-ing. Transition is the result of a transfer of awareness (consciousness) that causes reality to be transformed.

I believe the Spirit of the Almighty via transference is the process by which our emotions shift resulting from grander thought alterations whereas consciousness is heightened. Our thoughts are merely potential energy. Those same thoughts, according to the perception of time, cause our feelings to run up and down the sides of both fear and peace as our beliefs are amplified. As a spiritual leader, I have observed many transformations. Let's look at this from the view of human beings. As people transition with purer awareness, they transform their character and appearance.

This has been the theory that most spiritually minded leaders have understood. Clearly, the transition element is within us as the highest beings on earth. Jesus, like other great spiritual leaders, has attested to this inner power belonging to the *soul*. From the view point of our *soul,* the act of passing from death to life or from a void state to an awakened state is how human beings experience transcendence. Morality, therefore, can remain forever transitory, and human beings can ever strive to attain its victorious height.

While there are various facets of human transcendence, we can perfect our inner selves by shedding fragile morality as we propel to grander realities. The prophets of old were in such harmony with this notion and, therefore, experienced accomplishments of the miraculous power to accomplish awesome happenings that we know and read about on the pages of history. Equally important, transition suggests that the nature of human beings becomes more likely befitting divine standards.

For there to be heightened morality passed along and super values to enhance the way that we behave, we must assume the responsibility of the inner self aided by awareness of the Spirit of the Almighty. Heightened morality creates majestic levels of human morals and, therefore, the source for behaving and interacting. To fully awaken to heightened morality is not the work of medicine and drugs, but deeply tapping into the inner self and its divine strength. As such, this maturity is the very work of what I have termed transition. Transition implies that the mind be opened to replace the previous thoughts that limited it. Learning to believe and understand that God is a Spirit that awakens within our human nature will help us to know that we can make all types of transitions as we are guided by this infinite power.

Mis-perception is the cause of transitory complacency. The Bible talks about salvation a great deal, but before it can take place within the heart and mind of believers, a transition from doom must first be replaced by faith in reconciliation. It is then that the realization of justification can alter the once identity of doom to another identity of oneness. Consequently, believing that past deeds are forgiven by Christ's finished work will be your experience of true transition. This is the first miracle of Christianity.

The wholesomeness here denotes deliverance from one state of mind to another and being saved from a previous state of mind perceived as doom to another perceived as a purer reality of the soul's eternity. This transitive morality is the substance that Christianity embraces. When the occurrence of salvation is perceived, it being *transitive morality,* the result is one's readiness to experience change of inward beliefs. Transitive morality, then, is not a natural occurrence at birth; instead, it is a willingness to open oneself to observe the internal learning process.

Morality and Transition

For this reason, the human being's experiences with life are a foundation that provides wisdom. It is worth examining closer in terms of having divine morality reflected before your eyes. In order that human being behavior reaches its peak, transformation and reception thereof are necessary. They both happen as you progress in regaining the authority of your life from those earlier modifications that were a part of your mind. It is then that transitive morality guides you in ways that holistically improve your being. I might add, this transitive morality awakens within you new perspective. To put it simply, *morality is reality*.

Above all, *transitive morality leads us to act knowingly*. The changes that occur with expanding your morality are the result of a heightened awareness that is self-assuring as you reach infinite be-ing. Infinite be-ing expresses development of awakening your fullest potential. To attain a state of readiness of accepting responsibility for transitioning into the limitless being of God for which we were created is our responsibility. To fully understand being a limitless person, Jesus informs us to believe all things to be possible.

Although to some degree, fully aligning the *human being capability* is a journey that requires possessing an evolving mind instead of a closed mind. When being taught by the Spirit of the Almighty, you encounter changes in your morality that demands an inner choice of new wisdom to indwell you.

Putting the thoughts together with the purest knowing how those same thoughts are understood is the same as giving meaning to the existence of those thoughts with the single faith to believe them, I acknowledge to be the determining source of evidence behind each discovery.

Dwayne Gavin

3
Morality and Spirituality

You may close the distance between be-ing enlightened and be-ing not awakened if you understand that your actions are the result of spirituality.

    Spirituality attributes to morality in a very relevant way. Many people have some idea about what spirituality is; however, there are four realms that I believe make up spirituality. To me, it is partly *imaginary*, partly *awareness*, partly *belief*, and partly *intent*. These factors are completely creative. Without one or more of these factors, to some degree, an explanation of spirituality would be void.
    As a little boy, I understood spirituality when no one had ever explained it to me. When I was seven years old, my mother

instructed me how to pray. She simply said, "Repeat after me these words, *'Now I lay me down to sleep, I pray the Lord my soul to keep. If I should die before I wake, I pray the Lord my soul to take'.*" The beginning of my spirituality had taken place within me. Those tranquil words had an enormous impact on me. Four things were awakened within me immediately after I learned this prayer: imagination, awareness, belief, and intent. Little did I know I was in tune with spirituality at the tender age of seven.

Here is how I explain the meaning of my understanding of spirituality. First, the words of the prayer led me to imagine Someone, God, Who would be assuring to me. I had to conceptualize the meaning of God, someone or something more assuring or greater than I. Yes, I would later have to search for more knowledge of God; thus, it would begin my life-long journey, spiritually speaking, to know God. Nevertheless, my imagination was in motion to create a Source of Power to which I could be assured of taking care of my soul. This was the birth of my imagination.

Second, I began to realize that within me, there was a field where awareness needed to exist. As I delved into the idea of imagining God as an assuring Source, my spirituality expanded because I then needed to describe Him. That is when my awareness was born. I thought, "What a powerful thing!" *Imagination has no way of limiting you.* Only you can restrict awareness by acknowledging what you give limitation. I knew this was another source with which to create for me the description of God, especially since I then needed to know all about God.

Third, I began to contemplate how God, in a spiritual sense, could ever be understood by me and others with whom I would share. Quickly, something, that I had not noticed, happened as I repeated in the prayer, *"...if I should die before I wake, I pray the Lord my soul to take."* From deep within my imagination and my new born awareness that allowed me to describe what I identified as God, I had to believe what I had intuitively grasped was the existence of God. *No matter the subject that we conceive, it has no existence except it be believed.* There is a simple saying of Saint Paul in the Bible: "For with the heart man believes unto righteousness and with the mouth confession is made unto salvation." Saint Paul is speaking to us today saying, if we can conceive insight and speak it, should we believe it, it shall be made a reality.

Individually speaking, *only what one believes is the actual meaning of the world perceived. In a very real sense, anything you co-create becomes impossible for you to separate yourself from. You are what you believe. At least for the moment, until you agree to accept change to your beliefs as your awareness is heightened, you are for that moment content.*

I am suggesting that belief is *mentally spiritual*. In other words, a renewed mind is the premise of something spiritually sparked. Unless we are transformed with a renewed mind, we cannot have a heightened spirituality. It becomes impossible to separate yourself from what you believe. As it is the condition for salvation, this principle applies to everything *mentally spiritual*.

Thus, belief gives existence and life to the things we hold to be true within our hearts. Belief and unbelief being what you consciously identify as evident regulate your reality. To some degree, again, belief is based on one's intention and cannot be otherwise. Think of intention as another way of having hope.

This brings me to my fourth factor of spirituality, *intention*. Going back to the tranquil prayer, there is one other part of it that I had to know if I were to understand spirituality as partly intention, it being the first words of the prayer, "Now I lay me down to sleep...." This suggested to me that I alone was to create the intention before anything else could take place. I had to create the occurrence of these things happening before entering into sleep.

A life of spirituality begins with intent. Make the intent and you will find out that your perception, your view, will unite with your imagination and give rise to awareness. Thus, should these factors be believed, all things are possible.

The Master Teacher Jesus Christ based all of His miraculous happenings on the foundation of believing. To some degree, it is not questionable to me that Jesus Christ termed unbelief as the inception of sin. Many people have mistaken their shortcomings by blaming something or someone. The only hindrance to spirituality is oneself. This also applies to salvation. Although some things are indicators that attempt to deceive you in life, they are not the most vicious extremes that distract you. The most common distraction from spirituality is not being accountable for your own actions.

Spirituality begins in the mind; therefore, a spirit-filled life has its origin in a spiritual mind. Spiritual mindedness is a spiritual life in abundance. Deception and misconception commence in the mind; thus, what one holds to be true is the greatest defense to any opposing perspective should that perspective intend to destabilize what is good for you. This is ideal for be-ing.

I would like for you to think of the word faith as a type of magic shield to cover your belief from opposing intentions. Faith is assurance, being confident beyond doubt of any sort; hence, it protects and holds in place your beliefs. The durability of morality is to disallow the extraneous extremes of the lack of self empowerment to exist in your mind. Never allow yourself to yield to beguiling conundrums that embrace and/or render you helpless. Always maintain the liberty that you are both justified and condemned by what you believe and/or disbelieve. Do not put too much emphasis on idiosyncrasies.

From a Christian perspective, I would like to bring Saint Paul to you again. Within most of his sayings in numerous epistles, the theology conveyed supported that justification of unbelief is by faith. Saint Paul says in II Corinthians 10:4, the weaponry of our warfare is mighty to the pulling down of strongholds, this being faith in what you believe. Here it pertains to justification for those who believe in Christ for salvation.

Christ has already felt and become degradation, embarrassment, shame, and humiliation for your sins. He has taken them out of the way, superseding your having to deal with them. In other words, the shortcoming of our deeds has been buried with Christ. Likewise we should understand that our be-ing has been spiritually resurrected with Him, and there is no need to attempt to do what Christ has already done. To do so suggests that we have fallen short of belief in Christ for salvation and taken it on as an independent assignment of our own, which is destined to fail!

Here, mature believers in Christ understand that He has taken out of the way their mentality of disgrace for shortcomings. To this end, salvation denotes the brand of morality that excludes embarrassment, disgrace, dishonor, and shame, for our lives are hidden in Christ and His victory. The morality for ideal be-ing is the mentality synonymous with salvation in its totality.

The essence of a person is what makes the person what he or she is and the reflection on how we live is the morality of our spirituality. Therefore questions about right or wrong, good or bad, ought and ought not are taken to the hands of spirituality.

Dwayne Gavin

4

Morality and Prayer

All the ways to being understood and getting understanding have been discovered in prayer and meditation.

Great emphasis has to be placed on prayer when it comes to higher consciousness. Unless we understand prayer, we may not ever fully attain how we prepare ourselves for heightened morality. To illustrate what prayer is, I will be using one word to define it. Prayer is only the process in which to *commune*.

By this simple process, I have been able to research the number of insights about morality throughout this book. By communing with the deepest ideas on which to enhance my knowing how to best give a gift to the Almighty, all discoveries led me to communicate in the book the topics that could propel what I have termed the Self (soul).

Morality starts with the Self. For example, the idea of this book is to get you to commune with your Soul to discover what is sincere for you to the degree that your soul becomes the transmittable agent of awareness, and therefore, the foundation of wholesomeness. Communing with your soul begins with effective prayer and is supported by meditation. This is what I am addressing as prayer. The effective result of prayer cannot be anything other than transmittable awareness coming out from a state of intimate heightened receptivity.

What is more, the essence of prayer is an expression of oneself in such a way that one is readily and clearly understood. In the same way, as you pray to God, your intention has always been to be understood. There are many litanies, written prayers, which outline the concept. Moreover, the generalized purpose of gaining God's insights and being understood is the whole matter of prayer.

As you learn how to commune with your soul, believe me, you will discover that prayer changes you. It changes things from your point of viewing them rather than changing that particular thing. I do know that prayer helps people to change and, therefore, situations. This is likely because you are communicating your intentions as you convey information about a particular thing to God, Who resides within the Soul of every believer.

Constantly, we pray to God by exchanging thoughts, messages, or information in order that He will convey to our receiving awareness divine ideas with which to heighten our understanding and to rearrange things around us for us. I can tell you from experience that prayer is an interpersonal rapport. To know the work of prayer, just commune with your soul and then you will hear from the Almighty. Such abundant revelations, transmissions, and messages are the source from which heightened awareness is born. Another word that I used in one of the previous chapters is associated with prayer is meditation.

Based on the underlying premise to commune, both effective prayer and meditation have the same goal: to bring you to ultimate understanding. For this reason, to consider them akin may help you choose what works better for you. To form the positive, comparative, or superlative contrast, it is probably best not to place emphasis on postures in which to pray or meditate but the results, which are most important.

To the degree of reaching heightened awareness, we must incorporate time for prayer and meditation in our lives. Understanding is the skill attained through prayer and meditation. Also, understanding is the ultimate power to have in life. All the aims of religion, theology, psychology, and spirituality are paths that we believe will direct us to understanding. At the end of every inquiry that you will ever have, understanding is your goal. Understanding fills your soul with assurance. Prayer and meditation are concepts that assure you of feeling sure about how to know God. Prayer and or meditating inspire self-confidence.

When you are uncertain, prayer and meditation can be used to move your doubt. Insecurity is the result of a life devoid of prayer and or meditation. To ensure your mind of peace and rest, make your life one of prayer.

The preparation for knowing God is through prayer and meditation. There are so many wonderful insights to be granted as you commit your life to praying and meditation. There is a profound answer released when you pray and or meditate – *understanding*.

Beyond what your eyes can see and your mind can fathom, there awaits understanding. It is the counsel of communing with the heightened awareness through prayer and meditation that provides you wisdom and direction. The ultimate power of prayer and mediation is a sustained life.

To sum it all up, praying and meditating will help you to know God and yourself better; just try them. Maturing in God comes through prayer and meditation. I can personally confirm through my own discovery of God, these essential practices have become part of my inner being. The awe of this truth heightens morality and increases the conscious realization that I am never outside of God; He is always with me.

The awesome results of prayer and meditation bring tremendous insights which resolve any questions of faith. The amount of effort one puts forth to seek and act on divine awareness is the determining factor of being effective for healing and rendering one's needs. The more sincere one's search within themselves for God's support and direction, the greater the heightened awareness that will come and rescue them from the fear of being insecure in their relationship and understanding of God.

As you learn to commune with God through prayer and meditation, you will discover a heightened awareness is available as you listen to your heart, acknowledging what is true in your soul. Therefore, you come to understand that the witness of the Spirit of God is always present to guide and provide direction in our daily lives.

The morality of prayer and meditation heightens our human perspective to the degree in which we allow God's leadership within us to transform our unconscious search for comfort into a full assurance that He will supply every good thing we need.

And this is the confidence that we have in Him, that, if we ask anything according to His will, He hears us. Whatsoever we ask, we know that we have the petitions that we desire of Him. I John 5: 14, 15.

5
Morality and the Inner Self

From birth one must start moving closer toward the sensational fire that burns in the soul in order that one comes closer to knowing what exists truly about oneself.

Living a life of happy pursuit has been the challenge of every soul. To begin finding the answers to the pursuit of happiness, *you must start with every burning fire of sensation that has always existed WITHIN YOUR INNER SELF. It is given the name "soul," being the house that the inspiration of the Almighty enters.* We will start with the soul, wherein lie the truth and the only answers for wholesome morality.

If there has ever been an inquiry of the mind, it is the soul inviting you to your truth about yourself. As you interact with the soul's invitation to examine what you may find within it, your answer of truth will always appear. Whatever you are ready to see, to know, and to find out, it shall be granted by your readiness to observe the inner self. It is here where morality is formed. Allowing yourself to be self-driven is a part of knowing what really satisfys you. To my discovery, satisfaction is a bridge to happiness. The happiness that I am describing is freedom whereas its opposite would be the torment of fear. Freedom is the source from which happiness comes.

This is the knowledge of the morality of your inner self, the intuition in your soul. No one can teach you the brand of truth as can your inner self. Trust always your inner person for the morality of truth that you hold. Moreover, growth and progression of morality tend to be darkened because of cultural beliefs instead of evolution of the self.

As soon as you are animated with the truth about why you are sincerely driven in all the ways that you are, change from fear to happiness is the outcome. The soul's giving birth to your morality of truth is the agent of transformation as it comes from understanding certain knowledge about yourself. This awakening motivates and empowers you to become happy.

One thing that I have learned from my theological studies is that there is no such thing as waiting for the world to change. The mentality of people in the world changes as the morality of individuals become the agent of changing how they communicate within the world. To believe that somehow you must wait for anything other than a shift in your thinking, perceiving, interpreting, and your beliefs about yourself and others become a distraction as well as a setback to quantum leaps toward becoming a moral being living divinely.

A change of understanding is the source of divine morality. Only by understanding what is within the inner self can you really perform at your happiest state because skills that enhance morality come from within your soul. What is more, morality takes on the very nature of the inner self and is consistent with

Morality and the Inner Self

the awareness of your true self. All in all, an aspect of quantum morality is the clarity of your inner intent. There can never be abandonment of happiness if you are connected with the component of your wholesomeness, that component is your soul.

In order for you to live in a state of appreciation and contentment, you must first consult with your soul. Second, you will need to get clarity about happiness. Third, you must realize that contentment is greater than any delight, and only the soul makes contentment a reality. Next, you should prioritize your thoughts not to be outside of what you are experiencing within your inner self. Lastly, you must allow your inner self to exhibit the morality that the true eye of your being sees. Life can be happy. As the soul is the part of your being that knows and perception really is a matter of identification, observing the thoughts and beliefs that hold you together will prove to be your edification.

Even though we are physical beings, we are formed by God's thoughts first. This emphatic thought is not melodramatic. It is truth. We are the product of thought. We were thought of by the Almighty and having the ability like the Almighty to think, our thoughts when acted upon in the natural birth process are the energies that cause life to happen. That is spiritual.

The soul within aids us in the awareness of freedom, perfect personality, perfect humor, joy, and emotional awareness. Let me explain more. Living by knowing the answers to your life means that you understand that the mystery of life is within you. All forms of knowledge come from the soul's intelligence; therefore, spiritual tendencies arise from looking deeply within and bringing into your inner self non-judgement about yourself.

To depend on the inner wisdom within your soul, your outlook changes from different viewpoints of conventional brands of happiness to a competent happiness that is limitless.

Nothing makes you happy like the freedom of your soul. I found these lines of deliverance by Jesus of Nazareth in the Holy Bible: *"I have come that you may have life more abundantly."* By this, He implied, let me show you how to live by being free. For instance, the best experience seems unknown yet the best experience is to be perceived. The greatest fulfillment seems distant yet, it is as close as your heart. Simplicity of understanding seems too good to be true yet, if God were in any way different, it would not be true.

The morality of the soul is silent; yet, it is very effective. One of my poems entitled "Silently Effective" says,

> *My voice is not loud.*
> *It does not have to be,*
> *But my wisdom is present*
> *Every day.*
> *All around me*
> *I hear of victory and defeat,*
> *And I remain discreet.*
> *Patience, humility,*
> *And being quiet*
> *Inform me*
> *When I have done enough*
> *For every one that I meet.*

The pivotal line of thinking suggested in this poem is that effectiveness can be demonstrated as a silent phenomenon. I think about the work of the soul when I am reflecting upon this poem. Many people are not willing to disengage from what is popular to silently investigate themselves quietly; whereas, I now delight in knowing what I am because of the awareness that my soul teaches me.

Morality and the Inner Self

Once I equated little holes in my pockets, ones that caused me to lose a few precious coins that I had saved, to gaps in understanding. Whenever I have not looked deeply at my soul for direction, I felt emotions over and over again that were similar to lost valuable coins having fallen through my pockets. Today, I will not wear a pair of pants should there be a hole in the pocket.

Too many people have not paid much attention to the gaps in their understanding that are open too far, preventing them from the real truth within themselves. Just as lost coins of value are costly when you need them and do not have them, so is quantum morality when you need to be free. You must close your gaps of lack of understanding by turning within. There you can find the thread that sews up the "empty pocket" of your understanding.

The conclusion that is impossible to know about your starting point to become intelligent is the beginning of finding your way back to your soul for confirmation, but this is not the way of proving that it is a true conclusion; instead, it is finding where your wholesomeness lives.

Dwayne Gavin

6
Morality and Reconciliation

The peak of your morality of reconciliation is in the experiences that cause you to become an actualized person, having developed a personality of radiance because of your expanded attitude beyond the hopelessness in your life.

Unless there is a real focus on a new way of interpreting our less-than-quantum consciousness, the empowerment of reconciliation would not be viewed as a means of interacting with this highest truth. Any time I have conceptualized the grace of unyielding love and its attempts to save me from living without freedom and well being, I seek to know the Almighty better. Because of our ever evolving lives, we simply must have the loving approval of someone to forgive us, love us, accept us, and give us opportunity to renew ourselves.

The Quantum of Consciousness of Being

Admittedly, I have not always known about mercy and forgiveness, which have always been a part of my life. After feeling ashamed for my ignorance about certain things as a young boy, the Spirit of the Almighty revealed some truths within me. To my surprise my very nature seemed to heal as I became deeply acquainted with the morality of reconciliation. Jesus of Nazareth says, "Ye are as gods." I take this to mean, as we are loved and put together by an Almighty Source, human beings have somewhat of the same ability. As I perceive myself to be forgiven by the Almighty for my ignorance during certain times of my growth, I had to learn how to forgive the world daily, including myself.

Thus, I began to realize that morality which heightens human being consciousness to quantum awareness was what is meant by being reconciled. It matters not if faith as to the acceptance of mercy, forgiveness, and love was or was not explained fully to me. After hearing the Gospel of Jesus Christ, I knew that I needed to understand how to quickly reposition myself after certain disappointments.

The morality of reconciliation changed my attitude and mentality about being condemned in situations to which I was connected. A complete story of human beings has to always include some form of reconciliation, along with a morality that saves from an endless torment. The love for humanity from the beginning of observing it shows that all live in the image of the Almighty with total access to Him. Subsequently, there could be no reconciliation morality should there be any exclusion of human beings living connected to our Source.

There is a spirit within be-ing, and the inspiration of the Almighty breathes upon it, assuring the possibility of reconciliation for which each soul may reach quantum morality. In one phase of my life, I asked the question, "What is the distinction between reconciliation and being lost somewhere?"

Morality and Reconciliation

I was answered by the soul within me as the Spirit of the Almighty taught me with these words: "You are already lost should you not believe that you are reconciled." For me, what a morality boost! From that point, I became a student of the Cross!

Reading the Old and New Testaments in the Bible gave me great solace. The fact is a morality that reconciles always positions persons to receive the transformation that heals the mind. Allowing yourself to see that the Almighty is always penetrating your mind, should you receive the wisdom of reconciliation that has been released for you to live, you will experience freedom of the soul and forgiveness of thoughts and feelings that trap you into condemnation. We are all put into our bodies to learn be-ing loved and to understand that the inspiration which preceded us is love; thus, our greatest purpose in life is that we understand that we exist within the quantum morality of love. The Bible has explained for us the morality of love we should exhibit: "Love suffers long and is kind. Love envies not; it is not puffed up. It vanishes not. Love does not behave unseemly. It does not exalt itself. Neither does it think evil. It is not easily provoked. It bears all things. It believes all things. That same love hopes and endures all things. Love rejoices in truth, and it shall never fail." Love shall never fall short of its mission.

The mission of love is being unconditionally compassionate. This way love exhibits no partiality. Love embraces every effort to cover up any temptation to resist behaving unconditionally compassionate. In all the ways possible, love surpasses any limit to restrict its boundlessness.

Think of love as a perfection of attitude. By seeing love in this light, we will be able to attain perfection of character, knowledge, and language. As we allow our partial willingness to be replaced with pure love that only truly is demonstrated in the ways that Saint Paul has conveyed, "We know in part but when that which is perfect comes, that which is done in part shall be done away." Love is impartial, enduring perfection. Total love is what has to replace partiality.

Love is the ultimate language. Also, love is the ultimate character and behavior. This is because love is timeless, boundless, limitless, and all encompassing. The morality of love is the motivation for increasing our understanding about how to behave perfectly. Though our work is cut out for us, the quantum morality of love is the standard of heightened morality. Love is seen as the best instructor for any lesson.

Furthermore, morality in the sense of reconciliation, when understood with clarity, suggests that human beings make endless efforts to remove the inability to forgive. They should remove hate from their conscious choice of interacting with themselves and others.

Deep seated resentment has to be acknowledged before it can be let go. Heightened morality that is superior understands that only forgiveness can release everything; hence, when the people to whom you have turned the authority of your feelings can be forgiven by you, you regain your self-control.

Morality that empowers you is the reality of pardoning people, places, experiences, and things. By doing so, you tend to rise above quarrels in your life. Certain times of your life cannot be forgotten until you recover from holding onto them in your heart. All attempts to develop the morality to free your heart from judgment eventually reconcile you at the same time. Learn to love this *ever- becoming self* for which you are responsible no matter the agony that you think others caused you. Really you can choose to exclude the reality of anything that you find improper in your life and so reconciliation cleanses you.

Morality and Reconciliation

So much of the character of Jesus of Nazareth has helped me to understand very clearly what it means to exhibit what He implied as *kingdom morality*. Jesus demonstrated the divine morality of pardoning every manner of accusation, and from His intent to them, they often contemplated a deeper knowing about the clarity of reconciliation. The answer for why it is best to be a reconciled person is simple: It renders peace within. It also prevents one from the expense of experiencing injurious heart emotions that are the issues of a disturbed being; thus, morality that excludes reconciliation is dehumanizing. No life can find happiness locked outside of reconciliation. All persons deserve opportunities to be redeemed. Unless you see it this way, reconciliation will not exist and a kingdom type morality will have been wasted. *We are always charting our destiny with what we inwardly approve as being credited by God. With this truth, God is within our being.*

As you take quantum leaps toward the investigation of God Almighty, you begin to discover something that I mentioned earlier in the book. That is, belief in God Almighty is to act in oneness with the infinite energy of God. There cannot be one without understanding the other in terms of relationship. Limitation to the proper morality of yourself and the Almighty is what causes separation in the relationship. You may reconnect with God at any time that you are ready to assess the relationship internally.

Until we evaluate our morality with an open-minded understanding and, therefore, take pleasure in going beyond the fear of knowing what does or does not exist within us, we will not conquer death and leave behind suspicion.

The Quantum of Consciousness of Being

Beyond the invisibleness of your senses, there is waiting for you the vision of hope and it is non-material. Only it is beyond what can be fathomed by our minds. Calling it the Spirit of God is my claim.

Dwayne Gavin

7
Morality and Clarity

There is nothing that can please the soul more than understanding and clarity about yourself.

It is always impossible to achieve clarity of morality until the restraints of doubt, fear, and suspicion have been removed. These little plagues have caused people to stray from the path that leads to *clarity*. There have always been true and false on each side of the coin of life. What has not always been comprehended is the clearness of how to rightly divide them. Morality is the essence of self-esteem.

There is a Biblical story that tells of a king whom fear had consumed to the point of doubting what he should do to clearly attain the victory over his opposition. You may recognize the story of the Prophet Elijah's being intimidated because he lacked proper clarity. He was moved by a rumor that someone wanted to take his life. Immediately, he felt he had little time to counteract the plot. In his haste, he became delusional and when that happened, he lost clarity, which resulted in a loss of self-esteem. Elijah's sense of belonging was wiped away because of his lack of clarity about the prediction of another person's ambitions.

After hearing of the rumor about his potential assassination, Elijah went a day's journey into the wilderness and sat under a Juniper Tree. There he requested that he might die saying, "It is enough now, O Lord, take away my life; for I am not better than my slain fathers." As he lay asleep under a Juniper Tree, an angel touched him, and said unto him, "Arise and eat." When he looked, there were a cake baked on the coals and a small container of water at his head. He did eat and drink.

Afterwards, he lay down again. The Angel of the Lord came the second time, touched him, and said, "Arise and eat because you will need strength to be physically able to make the journey." He arose, ate, and drank. Elijah had strength and endurance for forty days and forty nights because of his eating and drinking. As he arrived at the cave, he made himself rest there, and suddenly the inspiration of God's words came to him to encourage him, saying, "Elijah, why are you here?" He answered God by saying, "I am the only one left of my ancestors who have not been murdered by my enemies, and now they seek to kill me."

While running from the fear of assassination, Elijah experienced and survived many catastrophes including a great wind storm, an earthquake, and a volcano. It was in the midst of these ongoing events that through a small voice, Elijah regained his self esteem, his sense of clarity.

It is the voice of clarity that helps your morality take quantum leaps. Clarity of truth and falsity is the awakening morality reaching its height. Unless we see clarity as a technique attained

Morality and Clarity

in inner awareness, we can easily become bewildered. Overcoming any thing in life begins the closure of the gaps in your mind which may be consumed with fear, doubt, and defeat. Any time that you are in doubt, you need a new understanding to replace your old thinking. By seeing your life from this perspective, you gain different skills to reposition yourself as you regain self-esteem. Often, this process demands that you change the way you are accustomed to thinking. At the deepest level of morality and clarity, there is always a need for thought replacement.

Thought alteration provides an awakened understanding of how you are effected by the things happening in your life. The intention of clarity is that you begin to regain control of your identity, personality, attitude, and character. Clarity of morality then becomes a replacement energy that you need to be self-sustained in your crises.

One day while rationalizing my ministry to the church, I was enlightened about the central purpose of my calling into ministry. As a student of the Gospel of Jesus Christ, I had to take on His mantle. Jesus wanted His followers to have a heightened awareness. Likewise, I wanted that for my parishioners. He created an intention for them by using an ultimate awareness with which to convert their moral perception about reaching the height of humanity when dealing with daily. Thus, He trained his followers to be examples of a new brand of theology.

As in the case with Elijah, something happens when you are consumed with loss of esteem; you contemplate death or defeat. No matter the occurrence in your life, do not turn the authority of your esteem over to death. The story of Elijah is given to teach us how to rebound by the clarity of a still small inner persuasion to refuse defeat. I, servant of Jesus Christ, therefore, wanted to create that same intention for my parishioners which would convert their moral perception of reaching the height of humanity.

Understanding the morality of clarity means that you refuse to entertain the inner acceptance of other people's opinions and/or suspicions. The morality of a heightened consciousness removes all identity loss, panic, dependency on violence, and any relationship other than your very own identity of beliefs. So often, things that are mentally out of balance pull on self-esteem and, thus, interfere with superior morality and clarity.

In a very real sense, we must not run away from suspicion or threats rather than find a way from ever being threatened. This is the work that involves how you are arranged inwardly. With what comprehension are you sourcing your emotions that render you the picture of death as did Elijah when he wanted to die instead of defending the task of maintaining stable morality?

In the congregation that I pastor, I have often told people that regaining control over your oppressors means that you have risen above living attached to the impression of oppression. Walking by faith and living assured of the small, still voice of encouragement from within are patterns that can correct wounded esteem. Sometimes we must have no one in our company to hear the inner self prompt us to come in and take a look at what should or should not be within our souls.

Chances are that we allowed whatever is within our hearts and minds to have place there; therefore, we have the right to redesign ourselves as we had the right to construct ourselves in the first place. This, I believe, is being in tune with the Almighty and being like unto His image.

When dealing with clarity, by any stretch of the imagination, the subject of the role of faith surfaces. Before anything can become your driving force, your faith is attached to it. Where there is absence of clarity, there can be no faith. Faith is being assured beyond all doubt. If you have no clarity on a particular

Morality and Clarity

issue, you may have thoughts about that issue, but even then, thoughts about that issue are only projections. Clarity on awareness makes faith strong, eventually endeavoring to expand morality.

Faith, like belief, works from your inner acceptance as you assure yourself of what you accept to hold as your truth, to happen beyond what you can see.

They all stand beside me: philosophy, logic, rationality, knowledge, thinking and science. Understanding is my name. The starting point of any argument suffers without me. Also, I am the premise for satisfaction and clarity. Wisdom is my kindred!

Dwayne Gavin

8
Morality and Perspective

The world that is given to all generations to discover is to make sense of perspectives.

When it comes to morality, perspective, the point of view that everyone exhibits, has the bigger role to play should there be lasting changes to occur person by person. Morality is a great teacher. I have known since I was a little boy that something happens when you take on different perspectives.

Our perspectives are always shaping our lives and our world. There is one perspective which changed my life forever. You may know it: *"Let this mind be in you which was also, in Christ Jesus; who being in the form of God and thought it not robbery to be equal with God."* Equal in the sense of oneness and unity is our minds in connection with God. Christ was whole at all times, and His followers must be no different.

Simply, these words refer to a perspective we need to inherit while we yet live. No matter our interactions with things, we must take on the morality and perspective of being both physical and divine beings. The ideal that we can live on the earth fulfilled- mind, spirit, and soul-is mysterious. Jesus advocated that. No matter the changes we go through and no matter the trials that we encounter, we can introspectively imagine maintaining such wholeness beyond broken desires.

This reality reinforces wholeness forever. One way to view this Biblical saying is that you understand we are never outside of God, and God is always present within us. It is just a choice of realizing this. Any breathing being is something mystical starting with its source of creation. A broken perspective for any reason is an issue of feeling separated from approval of some sort. The perspective of divine morality is to understand that nothing is left out of the equation of your life. All that you will ever need resides within you. It is up to each individual to awaken the perspective of divine morality. Believing that such a perspective of the Divine can be your outlook is within your reach. To grasp this level of morality is to wear the perspective of be-ing in the form of God and not thinking yourself less deserving of being there. This is what Jesus meant. We are to humble ourselves because we are as God.

This suggests believing that your perspective of God allows God to be a part of your outlook. As a result of taking on the mind of God, we can, by thought, become energized to do the work of God being fully capable of transforming ourselves from one state to another state of heightened morality. Being able to see yourself as an instrument and having at least the infinite capability of imagining being used by God is to become aware of how perspectives shape everything in this big world in which we live.

Everything is a perspective. Anything that has or can be

Morality and Perspective

given meaning is the result of perspective. When we give meaning to the world, perspective is being performed. As we become innovative beings, our imaginations allow us to expand the notion of perspective as we use words like <u>sides</u>, <u>separate</u>, <u>two</u>, <u>differ</u>, <u>unlike</u>, <u>unusual</u>, <u>contrast</u>, <u>variety</u>, <u>comparison</u>, <u>contradiction</u>, <u>incompatible</u>, <u>inconsistent</u>, <u>conflict</u>, <u>clash</u>, <u>mismatch</u>, and <u>unrelated</u>.

The point that I want to convey is that perspective is a matter of recurring interests with which we gauge and/or predict facets of ideas. As we look beyond something considered as a whole, our perspective is at work.

Over the many long periods of meditation in my life, I became acquainted with how perspectives occur as a second process of observation. The first involvement of observation derives from interacting with an idea, subject, and/or image. Next the perspective of the idea, subject and/or image comes to surface; thus, the perspective is the result of interacting with an observation or giving meaning to an observation. Taking some responsibility for your perspectives in life is the quantum goal of enlightened morality. Basing everything on which you gauge your interpretation will help you understand the morality of heightened perspective and, to another degree, see all perspectives alike.

When using your perspective, be sure that you know it is yours only unless someone other than yourself accepts it. Then it becomes shared. The most vital lesson about perspective is that it is not a stopping point; instead, it can just be a point to agree or disagree. Perspectives are as lenses in a pair of glasses that someone wears. The epitome of the morality of perspective is that as your internal vision changes, your outward view changes. Likewise, lenses in your glasses often need to be replaced when your vision either increases or decreases.

Living with a short-range perspective decorates an idea, and living with a long-range perspective is part of a decorative idea. Both are part of an aging process as your awareness is enhanced. There is really no certain age or day for your perspective of divine morality to awaken; it is just a matter of knowing that time itself is a perspective. Listen as Paul speaks to us; "Let *this mind come to you* …." Your imagination of what it means to be equal with God is a perspective that will cause you to go beyond your physical ability.

In summation, you may be surprised to find out who you are, of what you are capable, and how well you distribute all things when you have taken on the perspective of divine morality. When your mind connects with God, you will find it to be like flying a kite. The higher you aspire to reach the human height, the smaller your vision becomes of the strings that once held you down. Learn to fly by imagining yourself a kite attached to no string; rather, know that you were born to awaken within yourself the perspective and mind of the Almighty.

9
Morality and Happiness

Happiness is reflective of your imagination encompassing the vast freedoms of making choices free from fear.

Always there will be something from which you need to break away in order that you become free. Most of the time a hindrance seems to get in your way of making the choice to be free and happy. That something is fear. Detouring from freedom of making choices detached from fear is what plagues you from living happily.

The vast freedom of your imagination encompassing thoughts independent of fear provides you the unspeakable admiration that your heart wants. Reflective of freedom is the wholesomeness that makes you happy. The morality of happiness is the thought of being empowered to give existence to the assurance that you are whole when you replace fear with liberty to experience every choice of your own.

Remember to respect yourself and not disrespect others in the process of pursuing happiness. When you are free to experience your limitless imagination and to act without fear, changes that enhance happiness occur within your be-ing. You suddenly realize how to be liberated from *false* evidence. Confronting *false* evidence is the challenge to happiness.

Long before I realized that fear was the plague keeping me devoid of happiness, I wondered if a happy life could be achieved. After a few encounters with the impact of delirium, delusion, and defeat, I decided that if happiness were to be attained, I had to erase the thoughts of making myself believe evidence appearing to be true. I had to realize that I was making myself believe things that did not exist. Certainly, if anything existed, I was the one creating its existence.

The morality of happiness is embraced with an ideology that is independent of accepting any persuasion that makes you feel as if you cannot be happy. To accept any persuasion that you cannot be happy is a setback to happiness. I tell myself often, "Sir, do not make things something that are nothing." For me, this reminds me that I am in control of what I create with my imagination that is all encompassing to everything that shows up on the inside of me. Now, I know that nothing is unhappy about life; rather, it is my perception of life that makes it happy or unhappy for me.

Another change that shows up when you practice living happily is you begin to appreciate life. Your life takes on a new meaning; therefore, you start to recognize the value and worth of a life of happiness. It is then that your new attitude of gratitude appears. Happiness is not the result of one thing. Instead, happiness is the answer to transforming the fear of being free to choose your experiences according to what you would have them as a result of being separated from fear.

After facing roadblocks to your happiness with the absence of fear, your personality takes on drive and ambition that empower you and everyone in your presence. We are ourselves the items that must be examined for there to be any meaningful happiness. Total awareness of our *be-ing* exhibits what is in our hearts wanting to be free. Every minute of supporting fear robs happy thoughts, and happy thoughts inspire imagination to act with innovation.

The morals and values of people that are happy are simple. People who find happiness in their lives have learned to capitalize on their imagination's intuition and willingness to follow it with respect of not restricting their happiness to other persons or things outside of their independence to imagine freely, think freely, and act freely. They also do not lose time going beyond fear wherever it is necessary to attain happiness. There is no particular science for happiness, but there is a particular requirement for happiness, and that is freedom.

Some major decisions are part of happiness. Decisions that are freely made are the components of happiness! If you place your decisions on anything other than choices free from fear you will eventually realize that you made the wrong choice. At the core of our being, there lies an awesome truth about happiness. That truth is being free from the fear of being judged critically. I believe that you will never criticize yourself for any choice that you make in life when you have followed your decisions to be happy whether they turn out good for you or otherwise. Consequently, you feel affirmed because you made the choice to follow your heart detached from fear.

The idea of being totally free to make your life into what you choose is the type of thinking patterns that will reward you with the happiness and freedom that your life can be. Persons free to see all the beauty that can be imagined are people who inhabit happiness and liberty.

Living by being happy is not a skill; it is a daily choice. There is no reason for anyone to be unhappy. Just by being responsible for your own perception of the world gives you the right to choose the world that you perceive. There is a Bible verse that is so intriguing about our having something to do with the world that we give existence: "God has set the world within the heart of man...." These words from King Solomon truly reflect his wisdom on the morality of happiness and making life what it can be.

It is your world to shape. Learn to be happy because you are the greatest influence of your world and the greatest contributor in the world. Happiness is a type of morality that cannot be totally defined but it can be totally yours when you make it yours.

We are always people in motion. Our happiness is constantly in the moment. Once we attain happiness according to choice, we, therefore, are content but for a moment, until the next disguise of fear makes itself present again. To some degree, fear will often exist wherever you have not explored. It is important we understand that exploring happiness is to accept being unconditionally free, knowing what lies beyond your present state of *be-ing* will always be part of our own perception.

Facing the unknown is the quest for freedom, and the discovery of freedom is knowing that you may experience what you have known. The thought of being able to feel happy is freedom, and whereas we are free to think whatever we choose, there are thoughts that can aid us to happiness.

Thought-conditioning is a practice that can aid you to a happy mind-set. Condition your thoughts to be thoughts that are pure, thoughts that are positive, thoughts that are not bound to fear, thoughts that are lovely, thoughts that are kind, thoughts that are honest, thoughts that are good, thoughts that are not provocative, thoughts that are not envious, thoughts that are not evil, thoughts that are not vindictive, thoughts that are not fearful, and thoughts that are not partial. The universal thought of happiness is all-encompassing, all-inclusive and all-supporting to a happy life. Happiness is the flavor of freedom of thinking, freedom of acting, freedom of choosing, and freedom of adventure.

The grander thoughts are bearing all, enduring all, and forgiving all unconditionally. If there were any words that I could use to make you see yourself being happy, these are they: *"You only can live here happy if you want to be happy; therefore, take responsibility and accountability holistically for your own happiness."*

Happiness depends upon our selves. Different men seek after happiness in different ways and by different means, and so make for themselves different modes of life and forms of government. Happiness is something final and complete in itself, as being the aim and end of all practical activities whatever... Happiness then, we define as the active exercise of the mind in conformity with perfect goodness of virtue. Happiness is an expression of the soul in considered actions. To live happily is an inward power of the soul.

Aristotle

10
Morality and Death

Death is a sequence of thinking patterns deeply seated within the soul that disunites that soul from its connection with the present.

Death remains the most petrifying reality to comprehend. It is often perceived as demoralizing when someone that you have loved succumbs to it. Without the stigma associated with death, it can be understood differently. When death is perceived with terror, human beings mentally break down. During this experience, nerves collapse, delirium and tremulousness crush our being, and that destructive process separates us from states of existence.

It is important to accept death as a form of thinking patterns deeply seated within the soul that disunites that soul from its connection with being a part of the here and now. Although, the five senses often define now for us, it is important to know that a part of our being takes us beyond. *Death inhabits the mind that does not visualize beyond this world.* Our imagination is present, distant, and beyond our senses; thus, it is eternally a part of our soul.

The imagination defines death for us in terms of thinking patterns. Thoughts of the imagination have creative power including destructive implications, as implications of peace. Conceptualizing death becomes a matter of interpretation of your infinite beliefs as opposed to a physical absence only.

A more insightful morality of death can be equated to a simple equation of differences of thinking patterns. Thinking patterns apart from the physical world or material world are discovered imaginatively; hence, our imagination has no limit to which it can envision whether we are here or hereafter. In some divine way, our ability to imagine life beyond our carnal bodies is the transcendence of death. This perception leads us to benefit from death rather than misunderstand it or fear it.

We can conquer death by ceasing to interpret it as an end of existence, and perceiving our bodies as our whole being. Our imaginations are the infinite creative tool within our being that fertilize thinking patterns. As a result of the imaginative self/creative self being accepted as a part of our be-ing, death will cease to be a threat when we see it for what it is, another manifestation of life. The creative imagination and its infinite vision explain the distance of the strings of mortality and immortality. Immortality is the life granted to your conceptualization beyond the here and now.

These infinite projections of the creative imagination and thought about departure beyond the body-spirituality, limitation and creation help us to welcome the occurring changeovers that belong with life. It is vital that we realize the part of our being is the creative imagination and to some measure, cease

Morality and Death

preventing ourselves from creating death by imagining death as physical alone instead of spiritual and physical.

First, the morality of death, if viewed physically, ceases with expiration of the body. Concerning the body, relate to it sensibly and materially, but especially relate to it imaginatively. By so doing, you can easily discover how you may change your morality about death into non-tormenting images.

I have believed since my early conversion as a Christian that the picture of Heaven is to be found within ourselves while we are living physically. If Christians allow their beliefs of Heaven to be discovered here and now in the body, then they can only carry their view imaginatively beyond the limitation of their physical bodies. Most of what is to exist hereafter is proven while being here due to our having discovered it first by the birth of imagination. Imagination is composed of the being creating acts which conveys the soul's conception, no matter the kind of images.

Whereas our physical bodies do cease to function, our spiritual imaginations function beyond our bodily states. It happens all the time as we have been part of occurrences while not actually being there bodily. For instance, there was a little Baptist Preacher who once shared his dream of a world embodying equality and justice for all people. One part of the dream put him before the promise land to view it. When he awakened, he realized that he was still in America, but his imagination had taken him to the land of promise to view. Today, much of his dream proves to be very real. Leaving the body is one view of transcendence rather than death.

Beyond the body there is no death. Too many have had experiences outside of the place in which they sleep. What is more, beyond the body is the part of your imagination that is a real part of your existence while you are living physically. Every aspect of an occurrence beyond the here and now is beyond bodily and as a result, to be viewed as life also. Parts of all spiritual literature come to us by the people having connected with God apart from their actual bodies as they were tuned in and as they may have seen, heard, visited and/or connected with parts of life beyond the here and now.

Spirituality is present and beyond the body. Certainly, I do not hope that we would call this death. The morality of death is that the physical being contains life and death at the same time. Of course, this is another form of thinking.

There are miracles present and there are miracles beyond the body. Our very imagination is miraculously present and beyond present, and we all cannot doubt it. Spirituality is just a term to describe the changes occurring beyond the bodily state and the summary experience is the joy for when one tells the story of the supernatural occurrences.

To add a thought, limitations have no place within spirituality, the same way that our imaginations contain no place for limitation. At the core of our imaginations, we all possess a space of creation. The life that we live we have built, and no one is responsible for it but us. The morality of death is awakening and enlightening. We learn life as we change thinking patterns daily. Calling it death really is not so sad, and calling it life really is not so sad. It is only what you imagine that makes it happy or sad.

Should we someday learn to keep our eyes on both life and death and see them as semblances of oneness with which we exchange, then we can understand that all we have ever done is exchange place with body states and out of body states every day. I do not think that is very sad at all. Life is fascinated with death and death is fascinated with life, and they are one and the same reflection!

11
Summary

    Morality reminds us of how to improve our character and in a divine manner. When we are dedicated to living a moral life, we understand the depth of a higher morality to become influenced by divine consciousness and to be strengthened for the duration of lives no matter the temptations that surface to impede it. It is our will that determines what our lives will turn out to be and to a great deal of a fulfilled life, our morality is the equivalent to the attitude we have toward a rewarding life. We can not be bound when we understand that our morality carries us anywhere that we want to experience. Growing daily or staying in one place by our choosing.
    Our morality is the determining factor of many outcomes in our lives. To believe that our actions are the influence of something or someone other than our own morality and decisions is absurd. The idea of being knowledgeable about our actions is the science of morality. Morality is as a measuring tool to adjust our attitude holistically speaking. Every decision, therefore is part of an attitude about you, something or someone

else. Taking control of our morality is a decision to exercise our will to make improvements in our life and relationships with others.

When you come to terms with this knowing, it will help you to deal with where you are in life and where you can be in life. With a heightened morality; your behavior and attitude make quantum changes in a positive way. When it comes to morality and a godly attitude, *God does not work for us; instead, He works with us and through us.* The heightened morality is connecting with the Almighty and to a degree, the manifestation of His intelligence replacing our limited knowledge in terms of personality, energy and power.

Making good or bad decisions determines what you term to be good or bad according to your opinion. I have long believed awareness of wisdom, knowledge and understanding of the Almighty enables a person to make life changing choices when influenced moralistically. We must be ever willing to live with the outcome and the aftermath of our conduct and thus, the purpose for seeking the advanced morality influenced by the Almighty.

If we are ever going to reach our fullest capacity, we must first understand that divine energy is all about us and define it so that we may plug our morality into this form of energy that can manifest power to create an attitude of perfection. The sources of energy in which we are plugged determine the impact of the outcomes that support choices that we make. Every aspect of life is supported by energy. Energy is the essence of life because everything is energy; therefore, the outcomes in our lives are regulated by where we plug our behavior in terms of energy. Morality then has a greater role to play in terms of our exhibiting the best character.

Careful evaluation and adjustment of our thoughts activate the power producing energy in our lives that impacts our

Summary

morality and above all, works for our motivation. How to regain lost motivation in your life is very much in the path of your thinking. Should you have ever needed to regain motivation in your life, it was because there was a need for your thinking to be re-evaluated and realigned and thus, your morality heightened. Only where there is a need can anyone become motivated.

Your life can take on new meaning when your morality is plugged into the energy source that bring to surface the manifestation of miracles. The fact is that transformation of energy and energy renewal start with a renewed mind and so does morality start with a determined mind.

Once you learn how to identify your thoughts, perception, interpretation, and faith with energy levels, you can know the flexibility of the forms of energy that expand your morality and energize your life. One goal in life should be for you to understand that your morality impact the lives of others. Every decision you make resembles the picture of some thought that potentially or actually exists in our mind. Therefore, I believe that you should be careful with how you use your most skillful tool, the mind and the thoughts you embrace.

Phases with which your life are advanced or retained are the result of your awareness of mental activity and therefore, to some degree emblematic of the distinguishing quality of your morality that will determine the amount of virtue and individual wholesomeness in your life and the degree of excellence that you produce.

You can advance your life by taking a minute to ask yourself before making any decision as to where it will take you and what outcome is it associated. Spending a few extra minutes to evaluate which possible outcomes that could result from your conduct can help you avoid unwanted behavior from others. Morality, when heightened can be a tool that adjusts your own conduct and possibly impacts the lives of other people and in turn, their behavior toward you and others.

Having a readiness to choose to act in accord with the purest thoughts will help you fine tune your morality and experience the grander outcomes in your life. Learning to make choices out of your mind, conditioned with the vitality of divine energy, will produce the abundance that you anticipated would unfold in your life. It is always better, therefore, to condition your mind with thoughts that are not associated with injury. In many ways you should only make choices when your mind is conditioned properly before making an important choice.

Carefully analyzing your thoughts is a wise thing to do because all that your life can really be is the effect brought about by your thoughts. Your thoughts and corresponding actions are what determine your morality, and with careful observation, you want to watch them. You must certainly understand that your thoughts precede you. It is better that you be thoughtful with your life because without being thoughtful about your life, you can not exhibit the best morality.

The whole matter of morality deals with analysis of thought alteration, self awareness, and self actualization. Whatever the subject, whether happiness or unhappiness, the best way to handle it without a doubt is by completely understanding that our thoughts play a greater role than anything else when it comes right down to exhibiting the best morality.

One who becomes mentally disciplined to every aspect of an abundant life, and whereas our thoughts can merely reflect the life we choose, takes on the responsibility for what happens in your life in the now. Only the people who are open to the awakening truth about life can really live it to its fullest. Life can be almost as good as heaven depending on what time you find yourself aware of the heaven within you and your morality being a reflection of it.

12

Epilogue

I have been inspired by many persons in my life. Either I have learned lessons that have awakened me or I have grown by accepting everyone's uniqueness. Life is a journey that everyone born must take. It is filled with lessons that will embolden us to be the most knowledgeable persons that we need to be or life will defeat us if we approach it feeling life is unfair.

In writing this book, it was my hope that you could find yourself in some way or another and realize how fair and balanced life can be should you awaken from all of life's experiences. Many times I have envisioned what could happen if I never had known the truth about myself, and I have always gotten the same conclusion: I would be void of knowing the truth if I did not awake.

There are sequences in all of our lives that can best explain being awakened. You can realize this when you have overcome things having once held you in captivity. This is what this book is advocating as quantum leaps of consciousness to heightened awareness; however, some delve deeper than others.

Morality has been the subject that has fascinated me more than anything else my entire life. Still I have not lifted all that covers the surface. I believe that this book will get you to thinking about what is beyond the surface of your life. There are many more conversations to be had on the quantum consciousness of be-ing.

There is magic without a doubt in our consciousness being heightened. Human power is a matter of knowing how to bring out the best possible phenomenon, and I believe sincerely that the investigation on which human being morality is based releases that power. Each time that my morality expands, I can truly say that I am asked to look closer at the Greatest Power.

13
Morality Insights of Dr. Dwayne Gavin

1. Your inner self is the place where morality is born. Therefore, develop this by applying yourself to understanding and your consciousness to awareness.
2. Prayer and meditation make you consciously alert to insight provided by our soul. The answer to any question or need in our lives is always found in our quest for higher morality.
3. Heightened morality enlightens our souls to the answers regarding our destiny.
4. The moment you learn to closely observe and follow the leading of your precious soul, you gain wisdom for your mind to direct you with a heighten morality.
5. The component to wholesomeness is found in your soul; go there for truth.

6. Reality is sometimes a matter of what you can fathom.
7. Changing your life is a matter of un-restricting what you identify.
8. Subterranean energy lies within you.
9. Miraculous ability is a matter of consciousness.
10. The ability of God works within us according to our accepting an awareness of it.
11. A healthy opinion of yourself puts you on the path of being an accomplished individual.
12. There is a quality of being in accord with a system of ideas that improves morals to the degree we desire perfection!
13. Personal correction escalates according to our pursuit of heightened awareness.
14. The world changes around us when you change the perspective of what you imagine.
15. The prerequisite to attaining heightened morality is a matter of attaining unlimited awareness.
16. Life takes on meaning after you have conviction about what you hold to be true and evident.
17. You must move up the scale of awareness to discover new beliefs!
18. Belief does two things; it regulates reality and it takes on new discoveries of evidence.
19. The more you move up the scale of reality, the more you discover new understanding of things in life.
20. To believe makes things come alive within you!
21. The element of belief has all to do with your inner wholesomeness.
22. Awareness transfers morality!
23. Transition is the result of transfer awareness!

Morality Insights of Dr. Dwayne Gavin

24. Our thoughts are morally equivalent to potential energy!
25. Heightened morality creates majestic levels for your morals!
26. Transitive morality is the outcome of ones readiness to experience change of inner beliefs
27. Morality is reality oriented.
28. Heightened morality leads to acting by faith, expecting the outcome before your begin.
29. Putting thoughts together with the purest knowing those same thoughts are understood, is the same as giving meaning to the existence of those thoughts with the faith to believe them, and therefore, the source evidence behind each discovery.
30. You may close the distance between being enlightened and being not awake if you understand that moral actions are the result of spirituality!
31. Spirituality attributes to morality!
32. A person with imagination will not be restricted!
33. No matter the subject that we conceive, it has no existence except it be believed!
34. Belief is mentally spiritual.
35. A renewed mind is the outcome of knowledge spiritually sparked!
36. It is impossible to be separated from what you truly believe.
37. Belief is the evidence that regulates your life!
38. Intention is what you are hopeful of attaining!
39. A life of spirituality begins with intent.
40. The purpose of heightened morality is to disallow the extremes of lack of positive self-empowerment to exist in your mind.

41. Never allow yourself to submit to beguiling conundrums that render you helpless!
42. You are justified and condemned by what you believe or disbelieve.
43. The essence of a person is what makes the person what he or she is and the reflection on how we live is the morality of our spirituality. Therefore questions about right or wrong, good or bad, ought and ought not, are taken to the hands of spirituality.
44. All the ways to being understood and getting understanding have been discovered by prayer and meditation.
45. Morality starts with self.
46. The essence of prayer is an expression of ones self in such a way that one already knows he is readily and clearly understood by God.
47. Prayer changes you. It also changes things from your perspective of viewing them and moreover things change when you change.
48. Prayer and meditation bring you to the same result, ultimate understanding.
49. Understanding fills your soul with assurance.
50. Insecurity is the result of a life devoid of prayer and meditation
51. To ensure your mind of peace and rest, make your life one of prayer
52. The power of prayer and meditation is a sustained life.
53. The choice to make in your life is one that you know can advance virtue and wholesomeness in your life.
54. One must look to the soul to discover the sensational fire that ignites purpose to know what exist truly about oneself.

55. Your truth about your life and wholesome morality lies within your soul.
56. Your answers of truth will always appear when you look to your soul.
57. Whatever you are ready to see, to know, and to find out, shall be granted by your readiness to observe the inner self.
58. Allowing yourself to be self-attune is part of knowing what really motivates you.
59. Freedom is the source from which happiness comes.
60. A change of understanding is the seed of divine morality.
61. Only by understanding the inner self can you really perform at your happiest state of being.
62. The soul within aids us in the awareness of freedom, perfect personality, perfect human joy, and emotional stability.
63. The moral responsibility of love is the motivation for increasing our understanding about how to behave perfectly.
64. Morality brings a sense of reconciliation and when understood, it suggests that you make endless efforts to forgive.
65. Morality that empowers you leads us to pardon people, experiences and issues from our past.
66. Morality is the essence of self-esteem.
67. No matter the occurrences in your life, do not yield the authority of your esteem over to death.
68. Your morality is a great teacher.
69. Our perspectives are always shaping our lives and our view of the world.

70. Your understanding of what it means to be created in the image of God is the perspective that will cause you to act beyond your physical ability.
71. Happiness is reflective of your imagination encompassing the just freedoms of making choices free from fear.
72. Death is a sequence of thinking patterns deeply seated within the soul that disunites the soul from its connection with the present.
73. God does not work for us; instead he works with us and through us.
74. Heightened morality is the result of insight about the mind within your consciousness and brings awareness that transforms your identity from basic stages of human development to a new understanding about yourself. Therefore you must take responsibility for becoming the new creation God intends. This is the final view of the meaning of a heightened life.

I would love to share my thoughts on other topics and Christian books under development. We are continually scheduling speaking engagements where I share my on-going research and insights for self-help and personal growth.

For more information, please write to:

Dr. Dwayne Gavin Ministries
Global Christian Church
P.O. Box 624
Lake Park, Georgia 31636
drgavin@hotmail.com

Bibliography

Every Problem: ***King James Reference Bible***
Copyright 2000, Zondervan Publishing, Grand Rapids, Michigan, U.S.A.
Library of Congress Card Number 99-75836

Self Actualization: Toward the Psychology of Being, Third Edition
Maslow, Abraham H., 1968, 1999, John Wiley & Sons, Inc.
Published simultaneously Canada
ISBN 0-471-29309-1

Life:The Journey
Copyright 1954, Smith, Lillian Eugenia, The World Publishing Company, Cleveland and New York.
Library of Congress Catalog Card Number: 53-6643

Imagination: Law of Success
Hill, Napoleon, Revised Edition copyright 1960 by Combine Registry Company

Think and Grow Rich
Published by Random House Publishing Group
ISBN 0-449-21492-3

The influence of Awareness: The Essential Spontaneous Fulfilment of Desire
Copyright 2003, 2007, Chopra, Deopak
Harmony Books New York
ISBN 978-0-307-40772-6

Mastering the self: There is a Spiritual Solution to Every Problem
Wayne W. Dyer
Quill, An imprint of Harper Collins Publishers
ISBN 0-06-092970-7 (PBK)

The Book of Secrets: Unlocking the Hidden Dimensions of Your Life
Copyright 2004, Chopra, Depak

Harmony Books, An Imprint of the Crown Publishing Group, A Division of Ramdom House, Inc., New York

ISBN 1-4000-9834-3